ACT THE PART

THE WORKBOOK

LAURA MARIANI

ALSO BY LAURA MARIANI

Fiction

Gabrielle, from the diary of (The Nine Lives of Gabrielle #1)

A vivid portrait of one day in a woman's life through her morning pages.
The city of London during lockdown the background.

Non-Fiction

STOP IT! It is all in your head

The RULE BOOK to Smash The infamous glass ceiling - For women & young women everywhere — personal transformation & success 101.

The Think, Look & Act The Part Series.

Think The Part

Upgrade your consciousness and mind-set. Make winning a key part
of your life and business.

Look The Part

Upgrade your personal brand. Make presenting your unique Best Self a key
part of your life and business.

More non-fiction books and courses are coming soon. Keep an eye for new releases, giveaways and pre-release specials by checking at www.thepeopleal-chemist.com

You can also buy books and courses directly from the author at
www.payhip.com/LauraMariani

ABOUT THE AUTHOR

Laura Mariani is an Author, Speaker and Entrepreneur.

She started her consulting business after a successful career as Senior HR Director within global brands in FMCG, Retail, Media and Pharma.

Laura is incredibly passionate about helping other women to break through barriers limiting their personal and/or professional fulfillment. Her best selling nonfiction *STOP IT! It is all in your head* and the *THINK, LOOK & ACT THE PART* series have been described as success and transformation 101.

She is a Fellow of the Chartered Institute of Personnel & Development (FCIPD), Fellow of the Australian Human Resources Institute (FAHRI), Fellow of the Institute of Leadership & Management (FInstLM), Member of the Society of Human Resources Management (SHRM) and Member of the Change Institute.

She is based in London, England with a strong penchant for travel and visiting new places. She is a food lover, ballet fanatic, passionate about music, art, theatre. She likes painting and drawing (for self-expression not selling but hey, you never know...), tennis, rugby, and of course fashion (the Pope is Catholic after all).

www.thepeoplealchemist.com

twitter.com/PeopleAlchemist
instagram.com/lauramariani_author
linkedin.com/in/lauramariani-fcipd

CONTENTS

Introduction   ix
Preface   xiv

DAY 1: THERE IS NOTHING TO FEAR BUT FEAR ITSELF   1
The Monkey Mind/dump the c*** exercise   1
The fear process   2
3 things to be thankful for   6

DAY 2: WHERE ARE YOU NOW?   7
The Monkey Mind/dump the c*** exercise   7
The Overview   8
3 things to be thankful for   14

DAY 3: ONCE UPON A TIME   15
The Monkey Mind/dump the c*** exercise   15
A woman's place   16
3 things to be thankful for   19

DAY 4: WHAT ARE YOUR BARRIERS - PART 1   20
The Monkey Mind/dump the c*** exercise   20
Cultural, religious & family paradigms   21
3 things to be thankful for   25

DAY 5: WHAT ARE YOUR BARRIERS - PART 2   26
The Monkey Mind/dump the c*** exercise   26
The "good girl syndrome"   27
3 things to be thankful for   29

DAY 6: WHAT ARE YOUR BARRIERS - PART 3   30
The Monkey Mind/dump the c*** exercise   30
Who's a "good girl"?   31
3 things to be thankful for   33

DAY 7: REST, RELAXATION AND SOME REFLECTION   34
The Monkey Mind/dump the c*** exercise   34
3 things to be thankful for   36

DAY 8: REST, RELAXATION AND SOME REFLECTION   37
The Monkey Mind/dump the c*** exercise   37
3 things to be thankful for   39

DAY 9: SUCCESS IS A RELATIVE THING - PART 1   40
The Monkey Mind/dump the c*** exercise   40
What does success mean to you?   41
3 things to be thankful for   43

DAY 10: SUCCESS IS A RELATIVE THING - PART 2   44
The Monkey Mind/dump the c*** exercise   44
What does success really mean to you?   45
3 things to be thankful for   48

DAY 11: WHAT IS YOUR WHY?   49
The Monkey Mind/dump the c*** exercise   49
The Maslow Hierarchy of Needs   50
3 things to be thankful for   54

DAY 12: WHAT IS THE PRICE?   55
The Monkey Mind/dump the c*** exercise   55
Everyone pays a price   56
3 things to be thankful for   59

DAY 13: PERFECTION IS BORING - BE AWESOME   60
INSTEAD
The Monkey Mind/dump the c*** exercise   60
Wonder Woman does not exist   61
3 things to be thankful for   64

DAY 14: REST, RELAXATION AND SOME REFLECTION   65
The Monkey Mind/dump the c*** exercise   65
3 things to be thankful for   67

DAY 15: REST, RELAXATION AND SOME REFLECTION   68
The Monkey Mind/dump the c*** exercise   68
3 things to be thankful for   70

DAY 16: THINK OUTSIDE THE BOX: WHAT BOX? ACT   71
THE PART
The Monkey Mind/dump the c*** exercise   71
Fake it til you make it - Part 1   72
3 things to be thankful for   75

DAY 17: THINK OUTSIDE THE BOX: WHAT BOX? ACT   76
THE PART
The Monkey Mind/dump the c*** exercise   76
Fake it till you make it - Part 2   77
3 things to be thankful for   80

DAY 18: THINK OUTSIDE THE BOX: WHAT BOX? ACT   81
THE PART
The Monkey Mind/dump the c*** exercise   81
3 things to be thankful for   86

DAY 19: THINK OUTSIDE THE BOX: WHAT BOX? ACT   87
THE PART
The Monkey Mind/dump the c*** exercise   87
Mirror Mirror   88
3 things to be thankful for   92

DAY 20: THINK OUTSIDE THE BOX: WHAT BOX? ACT   93
THE PART
The Monkey Mind/dump the c*** exercise   93
Review time   94
3 things to be thankful for   95

DAY 21 : REST, RELAXATION AND SOME REFLECTION   96
The Monkey Mind/dump the c*** exercise   96
3 things to be thankful for   98

DAY 22 : REST, RELAXATION AND SOME REFLECTION   99
The Monkey Mind/dump the c*** exercise   99
3 things to be thankful for   101

DAY 23: THINK OUTSIDE THE BOX: WHAT BOX? ACT   102
THE PART
The Monkey Mind/dump the c*** exercise   102
Change is inevitable. Progress is a choice: challenge 1   103
3 things to be thankful for   106

DAY 24: THINK OUTSIDE THE BOX: WHAT BOX? ACT   107
THE PART
The Monkey Mind/dump the c*** exercise   107
Change is inevitable. Progress is a choice: challenge 2   108
3 things to be thankful for   110

DAY 25: THINK OUTSIDE THE BOX: WHAT BOX? ACT   111
THE PART
The Monkey Mind/dump the c*** exercise   111
Change is inevitable. Progress is a choice: challenge 3   112
3 things to be thankful for   114

DAY 26: THINK OUTSIDE THE BOX: WHAT BOX? ACT   115
THE PART
The Monkey Mind/dump the c*** exercise   115
Change is inevitable. Progress is a choice: challenge 4   116

Say YES some more.   116
3 things to be thankful for   118

DAY 27: THINK OUTSIDE THE BOX: WHAT BOX? ACT THE PART   119
*The Monkey Mind/dump the c*** exercise*   119
Change is inevitable. Progress is a choice: challenge 5   120
3 things to be thankful for   122

DAY 28 : REST, RELAXATION AND SOME REFLECTION   123
*The Monkey Mind/dump the c*** exercise*   123
3 things to be thankful for   125

DAY 29 : REST, RELAXATION AND SOME REFLECTION   126
*The Monkey Mind/dump the c*** exercise*   126
3 things to be thankful for   128

DAY 30 : NEXT STEPS   129
*The Monkey Mind/dump the c*** exercise*   129
All together now   130
3 things to be thankful for   137

One Last Thing   138
Author's Note   139

INTRODUCTION

Women on Boards, or lack of them, is still a current topic — if you are looking at top global companies worldwide women in leadership represent 12% of the total (depending on what research is taken into consideration and the number of companies surveyed).

International Women's Day has a pledge every year, and each year we go around the same merry-go-round, new legislation, new pledges, new campaigns and there we go again.

According to recent research carried out at the BI Norwegian Business School by Professor Øyvind L. Martinsen and Professor Lars Glasø, women are better suited at leadership than men based on five personality traits, which can be measured for effective leadership. The study surveyed more than 2,900 managers to ascertain leadership personality traits.

Women scored higher in:

- Initiative and clear communication;
- Openness and ability to innovate;

- Sociability and supportiveness; and
- Methodical management and goal setting.

So, if women possess most of the qualities necessary to be a leader, what is stopping them? Lack of visible female leadership and role models has certainly played a part, same as cultural and family paradigms, sexism, racism, ageism and all other isms out there.

Human beings throughout history, however (including women) have overcome obstacles that seemed insurmountable to achieve their dreams/justice or whatever it is they wanted during times when overcoming these obstacles represented everything that was "the right thing to do", during times when laws were against them.

Did this stop them?
   Of course not, they fought and found a way, because the what and why were bigger than the "No you can't".

There were people who accepted the way things were and conformed, still are, people that think that things are unfair, the state should do more, religion should do more, someone else should do more, always someone else.

You know what? It is time to STOP IT!!!
   Stop giving power to external forces and let them control your life.

STOP IT!

Smash that ceiling, and I mean the ceiling in your head, the only thing that is truly stopping you to achieve what you really want, and if that is being CEO of some company or Prime Minister/President or whatever, so be it.

My goal is for you to realize that, once you have truly come to terms with what you really want for your life and why you really want it, once you have controlled your mind and believe, you will be unstoppable.

I hope this workbook becomes one of the many steps taking you where you want to go.

Stop it! It is all in your head – Smash Your Ceiling.

Laura xxx

Why this workbook

I wrote my book "STOP IT! It is all in your head" as a call to action for women like you to take ownership and responsibility for their career and climb that ladder all the way up to the ceiling and smash it, if that is what they wish.

In my career as a corporate human resource director I had seen too many talented women selling themselves short and missing out on opportunities, not because there were none (there were and ready for the taking) but because of the way they approached the whole thing.
I wanted to help and break down the biggest barrier of all :

- Mindset.

I wrote the book as a practical, no-nonsense guide, with some exercises to start the process along and move people in the right direction.

This workbook, together with the other two workbooks "Think The Part" and "Look The Part", is the next step forward, transforming and enlarging your perceptions, and challenging and overthrowing some of your negative beliefs about yourself and your environment.

"Act The Part" (and "Think The Part" or "Look The Part") is experiential and motivational rather than informational.

What does that mean?

Very simply, it means that it works not by transferring a body of data from me to you. Its main function is to create an experience which will in itself and of itself change the way you see yourself.

As always, what you will get out of it depends largely on what you contribute to it and your commitment to follow through.

The workbook is also designed to affect the whole person and free up your capacity for self-expression, drawing upon not just the thinking analytical mind but also imagination and intuition.

It helps you to discover how your own personal belief system stands in your own way of success and then take you there, after you have truly decided where that is and why you really want it.

If you are frustrated, annoyed, disillusioned, you are going to project that into your professional and personal life.

Time to adopt airlines' guidelines — put your oxygen mask first and start flying free!

PREFACE

How to use this workbook

This workbook is part of a series of three (Think, Look and Act The Part) and was written both as an accompaniment and complement to the "STOP IT! It is all in your head" book but also a stand-alone self-discovery self-empowerment workbook and can be used in these different ways:

1. In combination with the STOP IT! book and the other two workbooks ("Think The Part" and "Look The Part")
2. In combination with the book
3. As a stand alone workbook

Option 1 - STOP IT! Book + the three workbooks

You have decided to go all in and immerse yourself in this journey, congratulations !!!

I recommend that you start by firstly reading the book in full (skip the exercises) and then start with the workbooks in sequential order e.g.

"Think The Part" first, then "Look The Part" and finally "Act The Part" (it all starts with the mind you see ...).

The workbooks are following the order/chapter sequence of the book with far more exercises of course (otherwise what's the point of the workbooks, right?), broken down into 30 consecutive days - 30 days to a more powerful self image and belief system.

Don't be tempted to skip through it and do more than one day at the time.

Instead of going fast, go deep into your feelings/fears and be honest with yourself.

And if you action one workbook at the time, and one straight after the other, you will go even deeper whilst also establishing some daily habits which hopefully you'll keep on-going.

When you go through the workbooks one at the time, some parts are the same: don't succumb to the temptation to skip the exercises.

Repeat them.

You will see that the second time around, you'll have different insights. Each time will give a deeper realization of yourself and release a higher and more powerful self image. And if you use them in the context/theme of the workbook (Think, Look or Act) you will get even more benefits.

Option 2 - STOP IT! + this workbook

If you decided to go with the "STOP IT" book and this workbook, again congratulations!

Again I recommend you start with reading the book in full , skipping the exercises and then proceed through the workbook one day at the time for the 30 days.

Option 3 - workbook alone

If you decided to go with just the workbook, still huge congratulations, a journey begins with the first step.

How to go through the workbook itself

The workbook is laid out as a journey for 30 consecutive days.

Each day begins with a Monkey Mind/"dump the c*** off your brain into a page" exercise.

Say what?????? You read it right: The Monkey Mind Exercise .

Put it simply, this is outpouring streams of consciousness on a page (or more) to start the day with a clear mind. It is a means to an end with neither right or wrong way of doing it.

I first heard of this exercise via Tim Ferriss in "Tools of Titans". He was inspired by Julia Cameron in her "The Artist Way: Morning Pages Journal".

Write a minimum of a page (you'll see, some days you won't be able to stop at that). I will just supply you with an opening sentence/word, a prompt and then you'll write anything and everything that comes to mind.

If you don't feel like doing it, force yourself: it is like therapy but free.

Each day ends with 3 things you are grateful for/appreciate related to the topic discussed for that day — it —doesn't matter how small and apparently insignificant.

Instead of talking about the usual suspects though (*grateful for health, children, the dog etc.etc.*) use this as an opportunity to review things in the context of the day's subject.

If you can't find anything to be grateful for/appreciate for that given subject, think again — you are not looking hard enough.

By looking for things to appreciate, you are firstly training your mind to look for positive aspects. Secondly, and most importantly, you begin to recognize how many more opportunities you/we, as women, have now compared to the past, many of which we take for granted.

When to start

You should really start on a Sunday (Day 1) with the "Fear" exercise to unroot your fears from the unconscious mind and bring them to the surface.

Owning and acknowledging fears is a very powerful first step to disempowering them. It is the fears that we ignore and that has power over us.

And then from Day 2 onwards, Mondays to Fridays, is reading and exercises — daily (we are talking about 20 minutes or 30 if you'll have a cup of tea whilst doing them).

This avoids the IDIOS fallacy . That is an acronym for *I'll do it on Saturday*, and it is a fallacy because a) you won't, and b) if you do, you'll hate it for eating up time in your weekend.

On weekends you are kind of free; I'm saying kind of because you should still do the Monkey Mind brain dump in the morning and the 3 things to be grateful for in the evening.

If you wish to re-read and go over the week, by all means do, but don't force yourself. Spend time resting, recharging your batteries , doing the things you love with the people you love (or your errands if you have to ...).

Time to start.

SMASH

YOUR

CEILING

DAY 1: THERE IS NOTHING TO FEAR BUT FEAR ITSELF

The Monkey Mind/dump the c*** exercise

P **rompt:**
    What comes to mind when thinking of the word fear?

....
....
....
....
....
....
....
....
....
....
....
....
....
....
....

The fear process

The fear process is one of the most powerful I have ever encountered; I discovered it when reading "Write For Your Life - The Home Seminar For Writers" by Lawrence Block.

I did it at that time and I have re-done it each time I start a new project/venture, both in my professional and personal life.

Fear contributes to our self-sabotage; it keeps us from extending ourselves and taking chances. So we need to bring it (or them) to the open and face it.

"Fear is the mind killer" - Frank Herbert.

Ready?

Ok, ready or not here it is — trust me; it is necessary to go through this.

I'm now going to quote literally from Lawrence Block's

"Write For Your Life" as the process is perfect as it is. It goes like this:

A fear I have about .... is that ....

1. If you run out of fears, make something up — even if you're sure it's pure fabrication.
2. Don't attempt to judge the reality of your fears. If something comes to mind, don't try to figure out if it really and truly applies to you. Write it down anyway.
3. If a thought comes to mind and it's so disturbing that you don't want to permit yourself to write it down, write it down!
4. Don't censor your thoughts. And don't waste time telling yourself it doesn't make sense; it's not how you really feel. And don't get trapped by the notion that writing down the

thought will make it real. The object of this process is to let go of your fears, and you let go of them by releasing them from your mind and putting them down on the page.

Write as quickly as possible, following the process. Do not stop before you've written down at least a full page (thanks again to Lawrence Block for this process).

Before you start, think about what brought you here, your professional situation and what you are trying to achieve.

BREATHE.

Breathe again.

Turn the page and start the process.

Go ahead.

A fear I have about .... is that

Take a moment to write down some things that fear has kept you from doing throughout your life — things that you really wanted to do.

....
....
....
....
....
....
....
....
....
....
....
....
....
....
....
....
....
....
....
....
....
....
....
....
....
....
....
....
....

Done?

And now, to move on from here write the following:

"I am now willing to act in the presence of fear. I hereby resolve that I will never again allow fear to keep me from doing something I genuinely desire to do".

Then sign your name and date it.

....
....
....
....
....
....
....

Name ....

Date ....

Enough for today — good job!

3 things to be thankful for

Think back at the topic covered today — what are the 3 things you are grateful for, despite everything? Remember, if you can't think of any — you are not looking hard enough. Think again.

....
....
....
....
....
....
....
....
....
....
....
....
....
....
....
....
....
....
....
....
....
....
....
....

You see? It wasn't that difficult, was it? Great work.

DAY 2: WHERE ARE YOU NOW?

The Monkey Mind/dump the c*** exercise

P**rompt:**
    What comes to mind when thinking of diversity?

....
....
....
....
....
....
....
....
....
....
....
....
....
....

The Overview

We cannot deny that boardroom diversity is increasing although women remain underrepresented. Looking at recent research from Credit Suisse more than 3,000 global companies found that women held 14.7% of board seats in 2015, up by 54% from 2010 (The CS Gender 3000: The Reward for Change, - 2016).

In the Morgan Stanley Capital International (MSCI) study, Women on Boards: Global Trends in Gender Diversity on Corporate Boards, November 2015, out of the 4,218 companies covered women held 15% of board seats up from 12.4% the previous year (73.5% had at least one woman director and 20.1% had boards with at least three women) while in the Deloitte's analysis of nearly 6,000 companies in 49 countries (Women in the Boardroom: A Global Perspective) women held 12% of board seats, of which only 4% at board chair position.

Research from many worldwide organizations have found that three women or more are needed to create a "critical mass", which can lead to better financial performance yet only 20.1% have at least three women.

MSCI found that having three or more women changes the boardroom dynamics and "enhances the likelihood that women's voices and ideas are heard", also resulting in better financial results than those companies who had fewer like 16% higher Return on Sales (ROS), 26% higher Return on Invested Capital (ROIC) and higher Return on Equity (ROE) than companies without (10.1% vs. 7.4%), as well as a superior price-to-book ratio (1.76 vs. 1.56).

They also found incidentally that companies with fewer women on boards had more governance-related controversies than average.

The highest percentages of women on boards can be found in the old continent with Norway (46.7%), France (34.0%), and Sweden (33.6%) leading the way and the lowest in Taiwan (4.5%), South Korea (4.1%), and Japan (3.5%) — source Credit Suisse.

Countries with specific targets, quotas, and penalties for not meeting regulations have nearly doubled the average percentage of women on boards including the aforementioned Norway, Iceland, Finland, and Sweden
(+ 34%) compared to countries without those measures (+18%).

Action Point
It is time to do some research and raise your awareness on this subject, starting from looking at the sector where you are currently working in, or the one that you'd like to be working in and progress, either or both.

Where are your customers based? Market/s?

....
....
....
....
....

What are the demographics of these countries?

....
....
....
....
....

Who exactly are your customers?

....
....
....
....
....

What percentage of your company/sector's customer base is female and what is the age range?

....
....
....
....
....

Now, look at the company you are working for or with, if you have your business: what is the employee's ratio of males to females?

....
....
....
....
....

What is the percentage of women in middle management and in leadership positions?

....

....

....

....

....

How does it compare to the percentage of men in middle management and in leadership positions?

....

....

....

....

....

How does this relate to your sector/company customer base ratio of male to females (I hope you see where I am going here…)?

....

....

....

....

....

Is your company male to female ratio at different levels or reflective of your market/s and customer base?

....

....

....

In February 2017 UN Women, a division of the United Nations dedicated to gender equality and the empowerment of women, unveiled The "Roadmap for Substantive Equality: 2030", in line with and supportive of the concerted global efforts to achieve the 2030 Agenda for Sustainable Development.

The purpose of the Roadmap is to repeal and/or amend discriminatory laws against women whilst ensuring that laws are supportive in general of gender equality & women's human rights.

The UN Women Roadmap for Substantive Equality: 2030 focuses not only in achieving legislative reform but equally, and more crucially, that they are put into practice.

The move from theory to practice, from the legislative framework to roll out and enforcement will require global coordination among different types of international and regional organizations, governments and so on.

The current estimate is that around 90% of the countries worldwide have at least one or more discriminatory law in their legislative framework with many different examples not exclusive to gender pay gap or women in leadership but also failures to adequately tackle violence against women, sexual harassment in public spaces and participation in politics. Gender-discriminatory laws are often rooted in discriminatory social norms, which remain pervasive and are difficult to change.

Action Point

List current social norms you believe to be discriminatory.

....
....
....
....
....
....
....
....
....
....
....
....
....
....
....
....
....
....
....
....
....
....
....
....
....
....

Great job!

3 things to be thankful for

Think back at the topic covered today — what are the 3 things you are grateful for, despite everything? Remember, if you can't think of any — you are not looking hard enough. Think again.

....
....
....
....
....
....
....
....
....
....
....
....
....
....
....
....
....
....
....
....
....
....
....
....

DAY 3: ONCE UPON A TIME

The Monkey Mind/dump the c*** exercise

P **rompt:**
  What is a woman's place?

....
....
....
....
....
....
....
....
....
....
....
....
....
....

A woman's place

What a "woman's place" is or seen to be has varied throughout history from warriors, powerful priestesses, and political leaders to portrayals inferior to men and I think looking briefly, very briefly (I'm not going to bore you with history and a historical portrait — it was not the purpose of the book and less than less this workbook) at the position of women at different points in history it can show us how our society has grown and changed and help us to understand the present, including barriers.

Women have gained and lost power at different times in history; if we look at back at the early times in Christian church, women could hold positions of influence equal to men, (even though the Da Vinci Code is a work of fiction, there are indications that Mary Magdalene was once a significant religious leader — an apocryphal gospel of Mary Magdalene was discovered in the late nineteenth century in Egypt – having a gospel in itself is of significance here).

The fourth and fifth centuries AD, however, saw the degrading of women in the writings of people such as Tertullian, Saint Augustine and Saint Jerome blaming Eve, and consequently by association all women, for the downfall of humanity.

The late 1500s is generally seen as the beginning of Modern History with the Renaissance. Yes, women were painted and portrayed beautifully, but this did not really affect women on a day-to-day basis.

A woman's place was defined as the homemaker with strict expectations: women could not vote and were discouraged in owning a business.

· · ·

Women of aristocratic families (with properties) were often forced/offered into political marriages where all their property then transferred to their husband.

The biggest gains in equality had to wait until the twentieth century, for example, with the Suffragettes successful campaign for women being granted the right to vote. World War one and two also showed that women could contribute to the economy and could work both inside and outside the home, taking men's places in factories.

The sixties and seventies and the advent of feminism further changed some of society's perceptions and, most importantly changed women's own beliefs.

Action point

Think back at three distinctive times in history — your choice: what was a woman's place in those times?

....

....

....

....

....

....

....

....

....

....

....

....

....

....

What did those beliefs mean for/translate to for women?

....
....
....
....
....

Find at least three heroines in those times that succeeded despite those negative perceptions/barriers:

....
....
....
....
....

What set them apart?

....
....
....
....
....

Shorter day today, good job.

3 things to be thankful for

Think back at the topic covered today — what are the 3 things you are grateful for, despite everything? Remember, if you can't think of any — you are not looking hard enough. Think again.

....
....
....
....
....
....
....
....
....
....
....
....
....
....
....
....
....
....
....
....
....
....
....
....
....

DAY 4: WHAT ARE YOUR BARRIERS - PART 1

*The Monkey Mind/dump the c*** exercise*

Prompt:
   What comes to mind when you hear the word barrier?

....

....

....

....

....

....

....

....

....

....

....

....

....

....

Cultural, religious & family paradigms

It is difficult to talk about religion without insulting/annoying someone somewhere and without being disputed on the interpretation/miss-interpretation of the scripture/s and this section is not meant in any way to be a pontification of the good/evil in religion/s and or the ultimate guide to mainstream religions's views on women.

This section is to recognize and acknowledge that religion has played/is playing and will continue to play a big part in the way different groups of people perceive themselves and others and their definition of "what good looks like" including women and their role in society and that there is a correlation between the two.

Many religions share the same characterizations and expectations of a traditional female role:

- Raise and teach children,
- Maintain a Godly household,
- Assist the husband decisions,
- Retain and care for family & familial assets.

I'm not saying that religion is the problem but mainly one of the potential restrictions. Sexism, misogyny and patriarchy and attitudes exist often entangled with other social and political factors and ways of thinking, including religion.

When I say patriarchy I mean a system of power relations between men and women, where men and women are complicit and agential, and which privileges particular kinds of gender and sexual identities (usually heterosexual men) over others. These power relations are part of the inner structural personal system with your entire personal image built on this — your belief foundation — which determines what you believe you can and cannot do, how should you do it and why.

Action Point

Now is the time to take stock and look back, not to judge and/or recrimi-nate but to understand and then move on: what effect do you think your own cultural background, religion and family paradigms had including your own reaction to those and how have they limited you-if they did that is (I know these are sensitive subjects, nevertheless, like an addict, it is time to face reality).

Be honest (yes, you need to do some work here :-)).

....
....
....
....
....
....
....
....
....
....
....
....
....
....
....
....
....
....
....
....
....
....
....

For women who wish to have children, there are also the obviously added barriers of going through the gestation period, the birth and consequent time needed to care for a newborn and beyond.

There is the physical barrier (not everyone has an easy pregnancy and is able to continue to perform to the same level/with the same intensity — the time-off pre/post — part) together with the childcare requirements.

Society is made of tribal congregations (religious and secular institutions, communities and families) all with their individual, sometimes divergent and sometimes mutually supportive views of a "woman's place", a "mother's duty" and "the right way of doing things".

Action Point

What are your inherited views about motherhood and a "mother's duty"?

....
....
....
....
....
....
....
....
....
....
....
....
....
....
....

Are these views supportive or conflicting with your desire for professional success and climbing the ladder? How so?

....
....
....
....
....
....
....
....
....
....
....
....
....
....
....
....
....
....
....
....
....
....
....
....

Gosh, that was heavy - You need a break for today.

3 things to be thankful for

Think back at the topic covered today — what are the 3 things you are grateful for, despite everything? Remember, if you can't think of any — you are not looking hard enough. Think again.

....

....

....

....

....

....

....

....

....

....

....

....

....

....

....

....

....

....

....

....

....

....

....

....

....

....

DAY 5: WHAT ARE YOUR BARRIERS - PART 2

The Monkey Mind/dump the c*** exercise

Prompt:
   What comes to mind when you hear the words "good girl"?

....

....

....

....

....

....

....

....

....

....

....

....

....

....

....

The "good girl syndrome"

Although there is definitely the outer game of society / family paradigms and so on, there is also a far more important inner game, your own perceptions, your own decisions, belief systems that drive behavior and choices made — the "good girl syndrome".

Rachida Dati comes to mind, the French Justice Minister under French President Nicolas Sarkozy who went back to work five days after having her first child by Caesarean section. Seeing her going back as what is perceived (by whom?) too soon started a barrage and ping-pong of comments and articles, some quite bitching and derogative and some alleging bullying from Sarkozy (and the worse ones were from women).

Even the way she was described ("impossibly glamorous and thin") had negative connotations (like what-all new mothers must look / are fat and frumpy??).

Better still, people were discussing if she is *right to put the demands of her career ahead of her child? Or is she crazy to miss out on some of the most precious months of her life? "* like there is only one way of being a mother AND a career woman at the same time.

Action Point
How much have your cultural/religious and family paradigms conditioned your views on what a "good girl" behaves like?

....

....

....

How much has it affected your career aspirations and/or choices?

....
....
....
....
....
....
....
....
....
....
....
....
....
....
....
....
....
....
....
....
....
....
....
....

Short day today — great job.

3 things to be thankful for

Think back at the topic covered today — what are the 3 things you are grateful for, despite everything? Remember, if you can't think of any — you are not looking hard enough. Think again.

....
....
....
....
....
....
....
....
....
....
....
....
....
....
....
....
....
....
....
....
....
....
....
....
....
....
....

DAY 6: WHAT ARE YOUR BARRIERS - PART 3

The Monkey Mind/dump the c*** exercise

Prompt:
   What comes to mind when you hear the words "bias"?

....

....

....

....

....

....

....

....

....

....

....

....

....

....

....

Who's a "good girl"?

Today we are going to delve deeper and this time into "your" idea of a "good girl".

Action point

Following from yesterday's exercises you should now have a good idea of your beliefs derived from the social/religious and family paradigms regarding the "good girl" syndrome (if you can't remember, go and take a look — go on .... I'll wait ;-)).

Now think back at times when you applied this "learnt judgement" and passed it onto others: go as far back or as near as you need to. Actually, I invite you to do so on purpose and see how and if your behavior changed with time.

Describe three different occasions at three different times in your life when you have demonstrated bias towards other women — or yourself — based on the learnt "good girl" syndrome belief (it is hard to admit, but we all do it and we all project our beliefs with our behavior — the point here is to have awareness).

....
....
....
....
....
....
....
....
....
....
....

....
....
....
....
....
....
....
....
....
....
....
....
....
....

How would you/could behave differently now, if the same situations arise again?

....
....
....
....
....
....
....
....
....
....
....

With understanding and acknowledging your own biases, you are taking step forward to a more level playing field — for yourself and other women. Congratulations.

3 things to be thankful for

Think back at the topic covered today — what are the 3 things you are grateful for, despite everything? Remember, if you can't think of any — you are not looking hard enough. Think again.

....

....

....

....

....

....

....

....

....

....

....

....

....

....

....

....

....

....

....

....

....

....

....

....

DAY 7: REST, RELAXATION AND SOME REFLECTION

The Monkey Mind/dump the c*** exercise

P**rompt:**
    Self-belief

....
....
....
....
....
....
....
....
....
....
....
....
....

This page is intentionally left blank

3 things to be thankful for

Think back at the topic covered today — what are the 3 things you are grateful for, despite everything? Remember, if you can't think of any — you are not looking hard enough. Think again.

....
....
....
....
....
....
....
....
....
....
....
....
....
....
....
....
....
....
....
....
....
....
....
....

DAY 8: REST, RELAXATION AND SOME REFLECTION

The Monkey Mind/dump the c*** exercise

Prompt:
    Time for self

....
....
....
....
....
....
....
....
....
....
....
....
....
....

This page is intentionally left blank

3 things to be thankful for

Think back at the topic covered today — what are the 3 things you are grateful for, despite everything? Remember, if you can't think of any — you are not looking hard enough. Think again.

....

....

....

....

....

....

....

....

....

....

....

....

....

....

....

....

....

....

....

....

....

....

....

....

....

DAY 9: SUCCESS IS A RELATIVE THING - PART 1

The Monkey Mind/dump the c*** exercise

P **rompt:**
    What comes to mind when you hear the word SUCCESS?

....
....
....
....
....
....
....
....
....
....
....
....
....
....
....

What does success mean to you?

Success means so many things to so many people; if you don't define what good (or great) looks like, you will be always chasing something, the next shiny object, unachievable targets and never be quite satisfied.

Action Point

Pause for a minute and think — jot down what is your definition of success.

....
....
....
....
....
....
....
....

Where does this definition originate from (family, friends, peers)?

....
....
....
....
....
....
....
....

Is this definition still relevant to you now? If yes (or no), why yes (or no)?

....
....
....
....
....
....
....

Has this definition changed in the last few years? If yes, what has changed?

....
....
....
....
....
....
....

What has been the constant (as compared to the variable) in your definition of success?

....
....
....
....
....
....

Well done.

3 things to be thankful for

Think back at the topic covered today — what are the 3 things you are grateful for, despite everything? Remember, if you can't think of any — you are not looking hard enough. Think again.

....
....
....
....
....
....
....
....
....
....
....
....
....
....
....
....
....
....
....
....
....
....
....
....
....
....

DAY 10: SUCCESS IS A RELATIVE THING - PART 2

The Monkey Mind/dump the c*** exercise

Prompt:
What do you feel when you hear the words GLASS CEILING?

....
....
....
....
....
....
....
....
....
....
....
....
....
....

What does success really mean to you?

Success means so many things to so many people; we have looked at what is your definition of success and how that has changed from a rational viewpoint. Now is the time to go deeper into your feelings.

Action point

Take some time to think about what success really means to you: a job well done? Position? Power?

....

....

....

....

....

....

....

How would you know you have arrived?

....

....

....

....

....

....

....

What is the feeling that success/THE job will give you?

....

....

....

....

....

What is really important to you:

- *Respect from colleagues / family / friends*
- *Financial security/money?*
- *Fulfilling expectations (family/friends/society)?*
- *Other?*

....
....
....
....
....
....
....

What is the destination and why? What will it give you?

....
....
....
....
....
....
....

What will make you feel truly successful?

....
....
....
....
....
....

How can you start feeling that now? Once you understand what success means to you, you can then recognize it and celebrate it — daily. Feeling successful, fulfilled breathes confidence — the more you recognize your achievements and feel good about them — the more confident you feel and the bigger things you will attempt, get my drift? ;-)

.

....

....

....

....

....

....

....

....

....

....

....

....

....

....

....

....

....

....

....

....

....

....

....

Great job.

3 things to be thankful for

Think back at the topic covered today — what are the 3 things you are grateful for, despite everything? Remember, if you can't think of any — you are not looking hard enough. Think again.

....
....
....
....
....
....
....
....
....
....
....
....
....
....
....
....
....
....
....
....
....
....
....
....
....

DAY 11: WHAT IS YOUR WHY?

The Monkey Mind/dump the c*** exercise

P **rompt:**
  What do you need?

....
....
....
....
....
....
....
....
....
....
....
....
....

The Maslow Hierarchy of Needs

Maslow Hierarchy of Needs is one of the best-known motivational theories trying to understand what drives
"Humans".

Abraham Maslow, a human psychologist, explained this concept in his 1943 paper "A Theory of Human Motivation" and his subsequent book "Motivation and Personality" stating that our actions are motivated so to satisfy certain needs.

Maslow suggests that people are motivated to fulfill basic needs before moving on to the more advanced needs, trying to understand what makes people happy and the things that they do/would to fulfill their needs.

His belief was that people have an innate need and desire to be all they can be but to do so they must meet first a number of more basic needs (the most common representation of this theory is often a pyramid, moving from most basic needs at the bottom to the most complex at the top).

According to Maslow there are five different levels starting at the lowest known as physiological needs.

The bottom of the pyramid has the most basic physical requirements including the need for food, water, sleep, and warmth, and once these are satisfied and people progress up the pyramid, and then these become more and more psychological and social, and so on, all the way to self-actualization, e.g., growing and developing as a person in order to achieve own potential.

Physiological, security, social, and esteem needs are what we would call deficiency needs, arising from lack and satisfying them is important in order to avoid unpleasant situations.

On the other hand at the highest levels of the pyramid are growth needs, which do not stem from deprivation, but rather from a desire to grow as a person.

The need for security and safety then becomes primary and it is all about control and order in our lives and consequent behaviors (financial security, health and wellness, safety against accidents and injury).

The need for appreciation and respect, e.g., gaining the respect and appreciation of others leads to the need to accomplish things and then have efforts recognized together with the feeling of accomplishment and prestige, self-esteem and personal worth.

Self-actualization - "What a man can be, he must be", is the need people have to achieve their full potential as human beings.

"It may be loosely described as the full use and exploitation of talents, capabilities, potentialities, etc. Such people seem to be fulfilling themselves and to be doing the best that they are capable of doing... They are people who have developed or are developing to the full stature of which they are capable," - Abraham Maslow.

Similarly to Maslow Tony Robbins, in his programs and many books, talks about in a more fluid & less hierarchical way the same drivers of human behaviors:

- Certainty and security
- Uncertainty and variety
- Significance
- Love & Connection
- Growth
- Contribution.

It is important here not to be too rigid about the standard progression of the needs within the pyramid: what is more important or indeed essential to one person might not be to others (except perhaps the basic physiological needs that are vital to our survival and essential to the survival and propagation of the species).

My point here is that, on top of the infrastructural belief system based on cultural, religious (or non-religious) & family paradigms, there are basic human needs that need to be fulfilled.

Action Point

This is a good time for a pause and to reflect: looking either at Maslow's pyramid or Tony Robbins's list which one/s of those need/s is/are the most important to you?

How are you fulfilling them right now?

....
....
....
....
....
....
....
....
....
....
....
....
....

What is your why (for that coveted glass/ceiling position)? Are you trying to satisfy your needs or responding to external expectations?

....
....
....
....
....
....
....
....
....
....
....
....
....
....
....

Refer back to your definition of success and what THE position/s would give you? Were you really honest (with yourself)?

....
....
....
....
....
....
....
....
....
....
....
....

You are doing great.

3 things to be thankful for

Think back at the topic covered today — what are the 3 things you are grateful for, despite everything? Remember, if you can't think of any — you are not looking hard enough. Think again.

....
....
....
....
....
....
....
....
....
....
....
....
....
....
....
....
....
....
....
....
....
....
....
....

DAY 12: WHAT IS THE PRICE?

The Monkey Mind/dump the c*** exercise

P **rompt:**
   What is your price?

....
....
....
....
....
....
....
....
....
....
....
....
....
....

Everyone pays a price

There is a perception that women (even more so women with children) pay a price to rise to the top of an organization/field , etc., (as opposed to it is easy for men?).

Let's face it:

Leadership requires 100% commitment – Everyone pays a price.

Action Point

This point is really important: if the "price to pay" for success/the position is perceived as "too big/painful" and/or unfair, there will always be an invisible barrier, like a force field stopping you from getting there.

Take some time to think what would be the sacrifices you'd have to make to achieve the top positions/dream job , etc.

Are they real or perceived? And, most importantly, are you willing to make them?

....

....

....

....

....

....

....

....

....

....

....

....

....

....

....
....
....
....
....
....
....
....
....
....

Are you making them too big? Are you self-sabotaging? If yes, what are you scared of? No BS here, we are all scared of something, write down your fears.

OK, done?

STOP IT!

Stop making excuses, It is all B*****t.

In the 2015 Global Entrepreneurship Monitor (GEM) Special Report on Women Entrepreneurship, women's entrepreneurship rose by 6% worldwide in the last two years.

According to the 2016 Kauffman Index of Start-up Activity, in the United States women make up 40% of new entrepreneurs (highest since 1996). In the MasterCard Index of Women Entrepreneurs 2017 (MIWE) women's business ownership across the 54 markets measured make up between 25-35% of total business owners.

On Day 2 – *Where are you now* — we have seen the statistics on women on boardroom representation according to some recent reports (respectively 14,7% Credit Suisse, 15% Morgan Stanley and 12% Deloitte using different samples). The barriers are the same including childcare.

And on that note, I'll leave you to ponder...

3 things to be thankful for

Think back at the topic covered today — what are the 3 things you are grateful for, despite everything? Remember, if you can't think of any — you are not looking hard enough. Think again.

....
....
....
....
....
....
....
....
....
....
....
....
....
....
....
....
....
....
....
....
....
....
....
....

DAY 13: PERFECTION IS BORING - BE AWESOME INSTEAD

The Monkey Mind/dump the c*** exercise

Prompt:
What comes to mind when thinking of perfection?

....
....
....
....
....
....
....
....
....
....
....
....
....
....

Wonder Woman does not exist

The idea that you should take as little maternity leave as possible, work until your waters break beneath your desk, never complain of sickness, swollen ankles and/or backache, and then go back to work fast and/or go back to work and (as much as you love your baby and being a mum) enjoying being back to work and more than baby-talk, but feeling guilty all the way through it, and then coming back home and be the "perfect" wife/partner/significant other (whatever you like to be called) and cooking, cleaning, tidying and putting the baby to bed is ludicrous.

Silence your inner critic — do you and what works for you.

Action Point

Does the picture described above sound like someone you know? Maybe intimately? What are the things that you do to please your inner critic?

....
....
....
....
....
....
....
....
....
....
....
....
....
....
....

The practicality of looking after a child, and who is going to do it post return to work exists and unfortunately, no matter the progress made recently, we can't deny that women, in the vast majority of cases, still bear the burden of household and family responsibility. That means women in general and even more so women aspiring to leadership positions have to juggle even more than their male counterparts.

All the employment laws on maternity, paternity, shared parental leave and flexible working mean absolutely nothing unless men take up/opt for these opportunities and support their partner/wife/significant other. It is easy to criticize "society", the government, businesses , etc., and ask for more laws, more rules to aid women coming back to work and pursuing a career/leadership and talk about what "men should do more".

Society is made of families and individuals and the change will happen and can happen — starting from your family and your partner taking up a fair share of childcare/household duties and so on.

Relationships do break up sometime but this does not nullify paternal responsibilities and accountabilities in raising children irrespectively of how much you might dislike/hate/can't stand your ex-partner and their new life (of course there might be fathers/parents who are unfit although let's consider this for argument sake to be an exception than the rule).

Think of your family unit as a business with 2 main shareholders whereby the decisions made are for the best interest of the "business"/family unit whilst not stifling ambitions and/or disadvantage either and/or both shareholders.

Too many times men request flexible working and or parental leave (and/or maternity leave) only and exclusively when their wife/partner/significant other already earns more than they do, far more rarely when they are on equal earning footing or thereabouts .The discussion needs to happen about your mutual ambition and career aspiration together with shared responsibilities and potential support needed (in what forms and by whom).

True feminism means accepting both the reality of motherhood, and celebrating its real value personally and to society as a whole but also having equal opportunities and being able to make a choice on how you would like to deal with your career and motherhood without having to apologize if you are ambitious and want to go back to work as soon as, or take a few years off.

Action Point

This is the time to look inside your own relationship – I don't want to cause breakups, nevertheless you know what needs doing here...

....

....

....

....

....

....

....

....

....

....

....

....

....

....

....

....

....

....

....

3 things to be thankful for

Think back at the topic covered today — what are the 3 things you are grateful for, despite everything? Remember, if you can't think of any — you are not looking hard enough. Think again.

....
....
....
....
....
....
....
....
....
....
....
....
....
....
....
....
....
....
....
....
....
....
....
....
....

DAY 14: REST, RELAXATION AND SOME REFLECTION

The Monkey Mind/dump the c*** exercise

Prompt:
   Forgiveness

....
....
....
....
....
....
....
....
....
....
....
....
....
....

This page is intentionally left blank

3 things to be thankful for

Think back at the topic covered today — what are the 3 things you are grateful for, despite everything? Remember, if you can't think of any — you are not looking hard enough. Think again.

....
....
....
....
....
....
....
....
....
....
....
....
....
....
....
....
....
....
....
....
....
....
....
....
....
....

DAY 15: REST, RELAXATION AND SOME REFLECTION

The Monkey Mind/dump the c*** exercise

P rompt:
Self-respect

....
....
....
....
....
....
....
....
....
....
....
....
....
....
....

This page is intentionally left blank

3 things to be thankful for

Think back at the topic covered today — what are the 3 things you are grateful for, despite everything? Remember, if you can't think of any — you are not looking hard enough. Think again.

....
....
....
....
....
....
....
....
....
....
....
....
....
....
....
....
....
....
....
....
....
....
....
....
....

DAY 16: THINK OUTSIDE THE BOX: WHAT BOX? ACT THE PART

The Monkey Mind/dump the c*** exercise

P**rompt:**
   Confidence

....
....
....
....
....
....
....
....
....
....
....
....
....
....

Fake it til you make it - Part 1

"Fake it till you make it" is a commonly used English saying which advocates that, by imitating confidence and/or competence a person can actually realize those qualities and achieve the results wanted.

"Fake it till you make it" does not equate to being a completely different person to what you are and/or being unauthentic.

It does instead mean, well at least for me in this context, working with some elements of your character, personality and/or skills that need practice and improving them to finally unleash your Best Self, both professionally and personally.

Remember the mind can be tricked — acting a certain way allows your brain to "rehearse" new ways until you have actually learned what you need to and turned into the real deal.

> *"If you're presenting yourself with confidence,*
> *you can pull off pretty much anything."-*
> **Katy Perry**

Action point

Let's look back at the Fear Process exercises on Day 1: how many different types of fear did you list? Was there a pattern by any chance? Describe the pattern/common thread.

....
....
....
....
....
....
....
....
....
....
....
....
....

Let's quickly recap on some of the things that fear(s) has kept you from doing throughout your life — things that you really wanted to do.

....
....
....
....
....
....
....
....
....
....
....
....

OK, let's dig a bit deeper now: can you identify the root causes for the fear/s? What are they? Again, is there a common denominator? What is it?

....
....
....
....
....
....
....
....
....
....
....
....
....

Write it down. List the specific aspects that you'd like to work on (for example confidence or self belief , etc., you get my gist here ...).

....
....
....
....
....
....
....
....
....
....
....
....

Good job, well done.

3 things to be thankful for

Think back at the topic covered today — what are the 3 things you are grateful for, despite everything? Remember, if you can't think of any — you are not looking hard enough. Think again.

....

....

....

....

....

....

....

....

....

....

....

....

....

....

....

....

....

....

....

....

....

....

....

....

DAY 17: THINK OUTSIDE THE BOX: WHAT BOX? ACT THE PART

The Monkey Mind/dump the c*** exercise

P **rompt:**
Behavior

....
....
....
....
....
....
....
....
....
....
....
....
....
....

Fake it till you make it - Part 2

"Fake it till you make it" advocates that, by imitating confidence and/or competence, a person can actually realize those qualities and achieve the results wanted.

Today let's follow on from yesterday's exercises and build on those, identifying three characteristics that you currently do not possess that are however necessary for you to achieve the next step in your career ladder.

I'd suggest looking at characteristics that are adjacent and complimentary to what comes natural to you to start with.

I follow the Tim Ferriss way of thinking — it is better to focus on your strengths than your weakness — this is because in working on your strengths it is easier and quicker to maximize the improvements and achieve greatness while working.

I know we are trying to "fake it..." here but baby steps here, baby steps...

Action point

What are your main strengths and talents (things you do extremely well with minimum effort, easily and enjoy)?

....
....
....
....
....
....
....
....
....

What are the characteristics that you currently do not possess but necessary for your next position/s which are adjacent to your main strengths and talents (A.K.A. something that stretches you a little without pushing off a cliff so to speak)?

....
....
....
....
....
....
....
....
....
....
....
....
....

Now think about how you could leverage your top strengths and talents to act out what you need to learn instead (yes, I know, you need to do some work here and think. It isn't called a workbook for nothing).

....
....
....
....
....
....
....
....
....
....
....
....
....

Next, what can you start doing right now to work on the characteristics that serve you the most (for the purpose of climbing the career ladder)?

....
....
....
....
....
....
....
....
....
....
....
....
....
....
....
....
....
....
....
....
....
....
....
....
....
....
....
....
....
....
....
....
....
....
....

3 things to be thankful for

Think back at the topic covered today — what are the 3 things you are grateful for, despite everything? Remember, if you can't think of any — you are not looking hard enough. Think again.

....
....
....
....
....
....
....
....
....
....
....
....
....
....
....
....
....
....
....
....
....
....
....
....
....

DAY 18: THINK OUTSIDE THE BOX: WHAT BOX? ACT THE PART

The Monkey Mind/dump the c*** exercise

Prompt:
  Mentor

....
....
....
....
....
....
....
....
....
....
....
....
....
....

If you want to be the best, you need to learn from the best – I have not invented this phrase — you can hear it for the lips of the most successful entrepreneurs, CEOs, billionaires out there. And that is the point.

You need someone who has been there, seen it, done it and got the t-shirt so to speak and you can emulate exactly what he or she has done and shortcut your way to success. This is applicable to both people you associate with on a daily basis and to choosing mentors to speed your journey.

"If you want to be successful,
Find someone who has achieved the results you want
And copy what they do
And you'll achieve the same results".
Tony Robbins.

Women may share a lot of things (the blogosphere explosion is a testament to this) but having a strong mentor usually is not one, men seem to be more apt at networking with purpose and connecting with people who can help them rather than just sharing experiences.

Having a mentor is one the most critical factors for continuous growth and accelerated success. Picking both men and women mentors that tell you not what you want to hear but what you need to hear is price-less: men will give you an insight in the way things are (if we are to believe the "old boys club" exists) and they can be an inside ally and advocate. Women can guide you on potential obstacles they faced specifically as female and how they dealt with them.

. . .

Action point

I'm not going to make assumptions so I'm going to ask you outright: do you have a mentor (or hopefully more)?

If not, why not? If yes, how have they helped you so far?

....
....
....
....
....
....
....
....
....
....
....

Thinking about the new characteristics you are trying to gain: what other/additional mentors might you need in the future? Ideally you should look for people who have the qualities/skills/attitudes that you are trying to "fake" in spade — they should be evident in everything they do.

(If you have already someone, don't feel like you are being disloyal — it is not just OK to have different mentors for different things, it is highly recommended).

....
....
....
....
....
....
....
....
....

What are the professional associations in your field/sector that you can join to both up-skill yourself and network? List at list five possible organizations.

....
....
....
....
....
....
....
....
....
....
....
....
....
....

Now it is time to look for networking opportunities to meet your new mentors and level up. Look up at least at two events per week for the next three months.

....
....
....
....
....
....
....
....
....
....
....
....

Now, think of specific examples of support/guidance that you need from your new mentor/s that would fulfill your need of "faking it".

....
....
....
....
....
....
....
....
....
....
....
....
....
....
....
....
....
....
....
....
....
....
....
....
....
....
....
....
....
....
....
....
....
....
....
....

3 things to be thankful for

Think back at the topic covered today — what are the 3 things you are grateful for, despite everything? Remember, if you can't think of any — you are not looking hard enough. Think again.

....
....
....
....
....
....
....
....
....
....
....
....
....
....
....
....
....
....
....
....
....
....
....
....
....

DAY 19: THINK OUTSIDE THE BOX: WHAT BOX? ACT THE PART

The Monkey Mind/dump the c*** exercise

P rompt:
Modeling

....
....
....
....
....
....
....
....
....
....
....
....
....
....

Mirror Mirror

Mirror, Mirror refers to the Neuro-Linguistic Programming technique of Mirroring and Matching to build rapport.

Mirroring is one of the most useful NLP techniques there are, is innate and even chimps use mirroring within their groups.

It is useful to determine whether people are visual, audial, or kinaesthetic (you do so by listening to their language patterns) and consequently adapt your presentation and communication/language style to suit the specific audience and have more impact.

State	Primary sense	Language patterns
Visual	Sight	I see; it looks good
Audial	Hearing	Sounds good; that rings a bell
Kinaesthetic	Feeling	That doesn't feel right; I can't put my finger on it

Mimicking people who display the required skill sets and behavior, even if you worry about appearing like a fraud is very helpful, according to research.

Professor of organizational behavior Herminia Ibarra wrote in the *Harvard Business Review* about such (her) research "By viewing ourselves as works in progress, we multiply our capacity to learn, avoid being pigeonholed, and ultimately become better leaders. We're never too experienced to fake it till we learn it".

. . .

Action point

Look back at the exercises you have done so far: what are the language patterns that you have used primarily throughout?

....
....
....
....
....
....
....
....
....
....
....
....
....

What those language patterns correspond to: Visual, Audial or Kinaesthetic? Is that what you thought, believed you were?

....
....
....
....
....
....
....
....
....
....
....
....

Mirror and Match practice = look at the mentors you have chosen that display the required characteristics (that you do not possess) identified as needed to move you forward. Start to Mirror and Match (be careful not to come across as parroting).

It would be useful to start with people that have the same language patterns you have (e.g., Visual/Audial/Kinaesthetic) — this will make it much easier and look much.

....
....
....
....
....
....
....
....
....
....
....

Plan situations when you can carefully observe how they "act the part" (the characteristics) and how they project themselves (with the language patterns). Schedule.

....
....
....
....
....
....
....
....
....
....

Mirror and Match practice = now look around and identify three other people that display the aforementioned characteristics but this time choose people that have the other two language patterns. Same "qualities/behaviors" but different ways of expressing; this will expand your tool kit.

....
....
....
....
....
....
....
....
....
....
....
....
....
....
....

As previously, plan situations and schedule them.

....
....
....
....
....
....
....
....
....
....
....
....
....

3 things to be thankful for

Think back at the topic covered today — what are the 3 things you are grateful for, despite everything? Remember, if you can't think of any — you are not looking hard enough. Think again.

....

....

....

....

....

....

....

....

....

....

....

....

....

....

....

....

....

....

....

....

....

....

....

....

....

DAY 20: THINK OUTSIDE THE BOX: WHAT BOX? ACT THE PART

The Monkey Mind/dump the c*** exercise

P **rompt:**
Act outside the box

....
....
....
....
....
....
....
....
....
....
....
....
....

Review time

Action point

By now you should have a clear view of your fears and root cause/s, your own personal barriers and definition of success, together with your what and why, know the price and decided to go for it plus three characteristics that you currently do not possess that you need to practice on.

Time to link them up...

....

....

....

....

....

....

....

....

....

....

....

....

....

....

....

....

....

....

....

....

....

....

....

....

3 things to be thankful for

Think back at the topic covered today — what are the 3 things you are grateful for, despite everything? Remember, if you can't think of any — you are not looking hard enough. Think again.

....
....
....
....
....
....
....
....
....
....
....
....
....
....
....
....
....
....
....
....
....
....
....
....
....
....
....

DAY 21 : REST, RELAXATION AND SOME REFLECTION

The Monkey Mind/dump the c*** exercise

P**rompt:**
   Being judged

....
....
....
....
....
....
....
....
....
....
....
....
....
....

This page is intentionally left blank

3 things to be thankful for

Think back at the topic covered today — what are the 3 things you are grateful for, despite everything? Remember, if you can't think of any — you are not looking hard enough. Think again.

....
....
....
....
....
....
....
....
....
....
....
....
....
....
....
....
....
....
....
....
....
....
....
....

DAY 22 : REST, RELAXATION AND SOME REFLECTION

The Monkey Mind/dump the c*** exercise

P**rompt:**
Failure

....
....
....
....
....
....
....
....
....
....
....
....
....
....

This page is intentionally left blank

3 things to be thankful for

Think back at the topic covered today — what are the 3 things you are grateful for, despite everything? Remember, if you can't think of any — you are not looking hard enough. Think again.

....
....
....
....
....
....
....
....
....
....
....
....
....
....
....
....
....
....
....
....
....
....
....
....
....
....

DAY 23: THINK OUTSIDE THE BOX: WHAT BOX? ACT THE PART

The Monkey Mind/dump the c*** exercise

P rompt:
Challenge

....
....
....
....
....
....
....
....
....
....
....
....
....
....

Change is inevitable. Progress is a choice: challenge 1

> *"Challenge yourself; it's the only path*
> *which leads to growth."*
> **- Morgan Freeman**.

The time has now come to go for it full on and practice the "Fake it till you make it" philosophy.

This week I will present you with one challenge each day to push your boundaries and getting you out of your comfort zone and practicing a bit more "acting" up.

Ready?

Ok, here we go...

Today we are going to tackle dealing and adapting to change, getting your mind (and your body) down a different path.

Beginning with small changes that do not represent a real threat, such as eating, drinking, sleeping, dressing and so on. The idea is to place yourself in new arenas where you control the interactions and practice doing things differently

Challenge 1

Make a list of the 20 things you do every day, your routines from what you do in the morning, what side of the bed you sleep in, the way you comb your hair , etc., etc. (I think you get the drift here...) to your evening routine.

Once you list them all, proceed to do something different for each and every one. If you drink coffee everyday, try tea (or chocolate or, God forbid, water!). If you sleep on the right hand side of the bed, try the left.

· · ·

Make it a game; you don't have to like the new things you are trying. You don't have to think about them or philosophize either. Just go down the list and do something different for each item you have listed.

And if you want to be really adventurous, don't pick the safe choice as an alternative but use this opportunity to do something really uncomfortable.

Go.

....
....
....
....
....
....
....
....
....
....
....
....
....
....
....
....
....
....
....
....
....
....
....

....
....
....
....
....
....
....
....
....
....
....
....
....
....
....
....
....
....
....
....
....
....
....
....
....
....
....

"The hardest thing to do is leaving your comfort zone.
But you have to let go of the life you're familiar with and take the risk to live
the life you dream about."
- T. Arigo

3 things to be thankful for

Think back at the topic covered today — what are the 3 things you are grateful for, despite everything? Remember, if you can't think of any — you are not looking hard enough. Think again.

....
....
....
....
....
....
....
....
....
....
....
....
....
....
....
....
....
....
....
....
....
....
....
....
....

DAY 24: THINK OUTSIDE THE BOX: WHAT BOX? ACT THE PART

The Monkey Mind/dump the c*** exercise

P **rompt:**
  Comfort zone

....
....
....
....
....
....
....
....
....
....
....
....
....
....

Change is inevitable. Progress is a choice: challenge 2

> *"The more failures, the more successes.*
> *Period"*-Tom **Peters**

Challenge 2

Dare to be mediocre. Fail on purpose. Yes, that's right. Today try something new and make a mess of it. In front of people. ON PURPOSE.

Describe what is the worst thing that could possibly happen.

....
....
....
....
....
....
....
....
....
....
....
....
....
....
....
....
....
....
....
....
....
....
....

Done?

Now go ahead and do it anyway.

Go on, I'll wait ...

....
....
....
....
....
....
....
....
....
....
....
....
....
....
....

OK, how bad was it? Anybody died? Non? I thought so ...

> *"It is not failure itself that holds you back;*
> *it's the fear of failure that paralyzes you."*
> **- Brian Tracy**

Things do not magically improve by themselves. You need to do something different. Act differently.

3 things to be thankful for

Think back at the topic covered today — what are the 3 things you are grateful for, despite everything? Remember, if you can't think of any — you are not looking hard enough. Think again.

....
....
....
....
....
....
....
....
....
....
....
....
....
....
....
....
....
....
....
....
....
....
....
....
....

DAY 25: THINK OUTSIDE THE BOX: WHAT BOX? ACT THE PART

The Monkey Mind/dump the c*** exercise

P **rompt:**
    What's the worst that can happen?

....
....
....
....
....
....
....
....
....
....
....
....
....
....

Change is inevitable. Progress is a choice: challenge 3

Say YES.

Saying yes means be surprised at what is possible and what you are actually capable of doing. Means being open and taking risks, and trying over and over until you actually succeed.

So say yes, and then figure out how to do it, learn and fail fast. And when you do that, you are the one in charge.

"If someone offers you a great opportunity but you are not sure you can do it, say yes — then learn how to do it later." - **Richard Branson**

Challenge 3

Start saying yes right now. Wake up and say, yes. Say yes to a project that is totally new for you and out of your comfort zone. And then over deliver. Today, start saying yes to a personal challenge .

....
....
....
....
....
....
....
....
....
....
....
....
....
....
....
....
....

....
....
....
....
....
....
....
....
....
....
....
....
....
....
....
....
....
....
....
....
....
....
....
....
....
....
....
....
....
....
....
....
....
....

The more you say yes, the easier it becomes.

3 things to be thankful for

Think back at the topic covered today — what are the 3 things you are grateful for, despite everything? Remember, if you can't think of any — you are not looking hard enough. Think again.

....
....
....
....
....
....
....
....
....
....
....
....
....
....
....
....
....
....
....
....
....
....
....
....
....

DAY 26: THINK OUTSIDE THE BOX: WHAT BOX? ACT THE PART

The Monkey Mind/dump the c*** exercise

P **rompt:**
   What's the best that can happen?

....
....
....
....
....
....
....
....
....
....
....
....
....
....

Change is inevitable. Progress is a choice: challenge 4

Say YES some more.

Richard Branson is a great fan of saying yes (apparently so much so, that he's nicknamed: "Dr Yes," among his Virgin employees). He says it's better to say yes instead of no because "opportunity favors the bold — this is a lesson that I learned early on, and have used to guide the Virgin story."

Challenge 4

Today say yes to a business challenge — even better: volunteer. Ask yourself for a change: what is the best that could happen?

....
....
....
....
....
....
....
....
....
....
....
....
....
....
....
....
....
....
....
....

....
....
....
....
....
....
....
....
....
....
....
....
....
....
....
....
....
....
....
....
....
....
....
....
....
....
....
....
....

The more you say yes, the easier it becomes. And the more confident you become. When you keep saying yes in business, people will be attracted to you and give you more and more opportunities.

3 things to be thankful for

Think back at the topic covered today — what are the 3 things you are grateful for, despite everything? Remember, if you can't think of any — you are not looking hard enough. Think again.

....
....
....
....
....
....
....
....
....
....
....
....
....
....
....
....
....
....
....
....
....
....
....
....

DAY 27: THINK OUTSIDE THE BOX: WHAT BOX? ACT THE PART

The Monkey Mind/dump the c*** exercise

P **rompt:**
   "May the odds always be in your favor"

....
....
....
....
....
....
....
....
....
....
....
....
....
....

Change is inevitable. Progress is a choice: challenge 5

Say yes, more and more ...

> *"Probably some of the best things that have ever happened to you in life,*
> *happened because you said yes to something.*
> *Otherwise things just sort of stay the same."*
> **– Danny Wallace**

.

Challenge 5

Today say yes to act, for the full day, like the person who has that fancy position you want. See yourself as that person. How would she talk? How would she behave?

Act as if.

....

....

....

....

....

....

....

....

....

....

....

....

....

....

....

....

....

....
....
....
....
....
....
....
....
....
....
....
....
....
....
....
....
....
....
....
....
....
....
....
....
....
....
....
....
....
....

"Do the one thing you think you cannot do.
Fail at it. Try again. Do better the second time.
The only people who never tumble are those who
never mount the high wire."
— Oprah Winfrey

3 things to be thankful for

Think back at the topic covered today — what are the 3 things you are grateful for, despite everything? Remember, if you can't think of any — you are not looking hard enough. Think again.

....
....
....
....
....
....
....
....
....
....
....
....
....
....
....
....
....
....
....
....
....
....
....
....
....

DAY 28 : REST, RELAXATION AND SOME REFLECTION

The Monkey Mind/dump the c*** exercise

Prompt:
  Self-belief

....
....
....
....
....
....
....
....
....
....
....
....
....
....

This page is intentionally left blank

3 *things to be thankful for*

Think back at the topic covered today — what are the 3 things you are grateful for, despite everything? Remember, if you can't think of any — you are not looking hard enough. Think again.

....

....

....

....

....

....

....

....

....

....

....

....

....

....

....

....

....

....

....

....

....

....

....

....

DAY 29 : REST, RELAXATION AND SOME REFLECTION

The Monkey Mind/dump the c*** exercise

Prompt:
    Empowerment

....
....
....
....
....
....
....
....
....
....
....
....
....
....

This page is intentionally left blank

3 things to be thankful for

Think back at the topic covered today — what are the 3 things you are grateful for, despite everything? Remember, if you can't think of any — you are not looking hard enough. Think again.

....
....
....
....
....
....
....
....
....
....
....
....
....
....
....
....
....
....
....
....
....
....
....
....

DAY 30 : NEXT STEPS

The Monkey Mind/dump the c*** exercise

P rompt:
Future

....
....
....
....
....
....
....
....
....
....
....
....
....
....

All together now

Now is the time to look back at the journey for the past 30 days, make some decisions and plan your way forward.

Action point

Describe your journey for the past 30 days — the good, the bad and the ugly.

....
....
....
....
....
....
....
....
....
....
....
....
....
....
....

What was the lowest point and why?

....
....
....
....
....
....
....

What was the highest point and why?

....
....
....
....
....
....
....
....
....

What have you learned about yourself?

....
....
....
....
....
....
....
....
....

What do you really (REALLY) want to achieve — the ultimate goal?

....
....
....
....
....
....
....
....
....
....

Why do you want it? What will give you?

....
....
....
....
....
....
....
....
....
....
....
....

What is your definition of success?

....
....
....
....
....
....
....
....

What price, if any, are you willing to pay?

....
....
....
....
....
....
....
....

What are the barriers you are facing to achieve your goal and how are you going to tackle them now?

....
....
....
....
....
....
....
....
....
....

Career mapping: your next role toward the ultimate goal (if not the same).

....
....
....
....
....
....
....
....
....

List the characteristics/qualities/skills you currently do not possess that you've identified as needed to achieve your career goal/s.

....
....
....
....
....
....
....

Describe the type of role models/mentor you need to support you in gaining the characteristics/qualities/skills and the steps you are going to take to start the mentor/mentee relationship.

....
....
....
....
....
....
....
....
....
....
....

Plan and schedule appropriate occasions for you to start practicing to Mirror and Match (Visual, Audial and Kinaesthetic).

....
....
....
....
....
....
....
....

Now reflect on what you have learned from challenging yourself.

....
....
....
....
....
....

Which challenge was the easiest? Why so — be specific.

....
....
....
....
....
....
....
....
....

Which challenge was the hardest? What did you find particularly difficult? Be specific.

....
....
....
....
....
....
....
....
....

How did you overcome the difficulty?

....
....
....
....
....
....
....

Now, plan challenges to "act the part" for the next four weeks :

Week 1

....
....
....
....
....
....

Week 2

....
....
....
....
....
....

Week 3

....
....
....
....
....
....

Week 4

....
....
....
....
....

3 things to be thankful for

Think back at the topic covered today — what are the 3 things you are grateful for, despite everything? Remember, if you can't think of any — you are not looking hard enough. Think again.

....
....
....
....
....
....
....
....
....
....
....
....
....
....
....
....
....
....
....
....
....
....
....
....

ONE LAST THING

You have made through the workbook: you should be proud of yourself for keeping up a routine that works towards your development and empowerment.

Now it's when the real work begins, if you quit now, you will miss the best part of your hero journey, the real adventure — when put into practice what you have learned and take action.

I would suggest you continue the journey with the next workbook of course. But whatever you decide, take action and follow through.

And, more than anything, remember these 3 things:

1. Perfection does not exist, Be awesome instead

2. Anything is possible

3. We are all in this together: if we can take care of one another, appreciate each other, we all gain — women inspiring and empowering other women

And when you start making excuses and blame someone remember:

STOP IT! It is all in your head,

AUTHOR'S NOTE

Thank you so much for reading and (hopefully working through) *Act The Part.*

I hope you enjoyed this workbook and it has challenged and perhaps overthrown some of your negative beliefs about yourself. A review would be much appreciated as it helps other readers discover the story. Thanks.

If you sign up for my newsletter you'll be notified of give-aways, new releases and receive personal updates from behind the scenes of my business and books.

Go to www.thepeoplealchemist.com to get started.

Bibliography

I read a lot of books as part of my research. Some of them together with other references include:

Write For Your Life - **Lawrence Block**
The Artist Way - **Julia Cameron**
Tools of Titans - **Tim Ferriss**
Psycho-Cybernetics - **Maxwell Maltz**
Self Mastery Through Conscious Autosuggestion - **Émile Coué**

Printed in Great Britain
by Amazon

83735019R00092